Transformation Workbook

Ruth Cherry, Ph.D.

Copyright © 2022 by Ruth Cherry, Ph.D.

ISBN: 978-1-990695-08-7 (Paperback)
978-1-990695-09-4 (E-book)

All rights reserved. No part of this publication may be reproduced, distributed, or transmitted in any form or by any means, including photocopying, recording, or other electronic or mechanical methods, without the prior written permission of the publisher, except in the case brief quotations embodied in critical reviews and other noncommercial uses permitted by copyright law.

The views expressed in this book are solely those of the author and do not necessarily reflect the views of the publisher, and the publisher hereby disclaims any responsibility for them.

BookSide Press
877-741-8091
www.booksidepress.com
orders@booksidepress.com

Contents

Introduction 1
Integrating your Vulnerability 5
Practicing Presence 27
Knowing your Inner World 43
The Controller. 63
Practicing Surrender 73
Consciousness. 85
Spiritual Warrior. 95
Partnering with Life 105
Your Sacred Duty 127
Practicing Peace 169

Also by Ruth Cherry, Ph.D.

Living in the Flow: Practicing Vibrational Alignment

Accepting Unconditional Love

Open Your Heart

Matters of the Heart

Matters of the Soul

INTRODUCTION

These pages welcome your soul home.

We all yearn to anchor in our own truth. We want to live authentically and meaningfully. We seek passion, joy, and self-expression.

These are our birthright.

But sometimes we lose our way. We're distracted by influences from outside ourselves. We trust our intellects to do work they were never designed to do.

We use our best judgment. And days pass and years pass and we realize that good judgment doesn't lead us to fulfillment.

We want more. Doing everything right isn't enough. And, so, we surrender.

When you reach that point and you throw up your hands and you say, "I must live deeply and passionately. Acting respectably isn't enough. I want to honor my heart's longing," then you open to transformation.

What is transformation?

Transformation is the process by which we recognize that we are human and divine and that our divinity heals and guides us.

When we allow transformation, we acknowledge that we don't know the limits of who we are.

We acknowledge our eternal center, the core of who we are. This arena of unlimitedness scares and entices us.

We dare to expect more of ourselves and of life. It is by moving deeply inside ourselves that we find the path we seek.

For each of us the transformative journey roots in our inner world. Paying attention to your inner world makes the seconds of your life sacred.

When we open to transformation in completely personal terms, we lose a sense of ownership about our lives.

The process of transformation is about practicing availability.

Life knows us better than we know ourselves.

When we commit to transformation, we trust life.

INTEGRATING YOUR VULNERABILITY

What is vulnerability? That word sounds ominous and undesirable. It makes us fear that we are weak, open to predation, unable to protect our boundaries, and not quite equal to others whom we respect.

In truth, vulnerability refers to living from our essence, the deepest core part of who we are. No pretensions, no self-delusions, no imitations. We simply be.

Integrating our vulnerability lights our soul's path home. We can move beyond our intellect's self-definition and beyond any concerns about competition or proving our worth. In the depths of our vulnerability, we know that we are worthy. We don't question that.

Integrating our vulnerability carries us to a space which our intellects can't enter. Our inner world doesn't present itself for examination under the spotlight of logical scrutiny. In fact, too much thinking stalls us. Vulnerability carries us into our eternal core where we participate in transformation.

Your soul beckons you home. Your intellect says, "No, thanks. Mundane reality is good enough." But you have had enough life experience to know that you want more. You want to be you, with depth and commitment and open-hearted self-acceptance.

And, so, you commit to this journey. Integrating your vulnerability is your first step.

Without pretense or need to hide, we simply experience what it is to be ourselves this second. No excuses, no amendments, no judgments.

This second I feel _____

Continue writing as you stay anchored in your vulnerability.

This second I notice _____

Continue writing as you stay anchored in your vulnerability.

This second I want _____

Continue writing as you stay anchored in your vulnerability.

This second I love the part of me that _____

Continue writing as you stay anchored in your vulnerability.

This second I distrust the part of me that _____

Continue writing as you stay anchored in your vulnerability.

This second I honor my _____

Continue writing as you stay anchored in your vulnerability.

This second I struggle with _____

Continue writing as you stay anchored in your vulnerability.

This second I appreciate my _____

Continue writing as you stay anchored in your vulnerability.

This second I imagine myself _____

Continue writing as you stay anchored in your vulnerability.

My feelings scare me when _____

Continue writing as you stay anchored in your vulnerability.

I've noticed that I close off my feelings by _____

Continue writing as you stay anchored in your vulnerability.

The bad thing about feeling my feelings when I'm alone is ____
_____

Continue writing as you stay anchored in your vulnerability.

The good thing about feeling my feelings when I'm alone is ___
___

Continue writing as you stay anchored in your vulnerability.

When other people cry I feel _____

Continue writing as you stay anchored in your vulnerability.

I avoid my feelings and others' feelings when I _____

Continue writing as you stay anchored in your vulnerability.

The hardest thing to accept about myself is _____

Continue writing as you stay anchored in your vulnerability.

I am comfortable with the part of me that _____

Continue writing as you stay anchored in your vulnerability.

I hate the part of me that _____

Continue writing as you stay anchored in your vulnerability.

I refuse to show most folks my _____

Continue writing as you stay anchored in your vulnerability.

PRACTICING PRESENCE

Move your attention inside by paying attention to your breathing. Notice the breath's gentle rhythm which continues without your conscious acknowledgment. What you need most — breath — is free and amply available. It requires no effort on your part to acquire. You simply receive.

Practice receiving your breath consciously today.

Write about your experience receiving consciously.

All day maintain an attitude of receptivity. Notice how that's comfortable and how it's uncomfortable.

Notice what you do to avoid receiving.

Write about your experience receiving and resisting receiving.

Receiving requires passivity. Practice receptive passivity.

What part of you resists passivity and receiving?

Write about your experience practicing receptive passivity.

In your inner world, move into your passive, alert Observer. The Observer stands behind the Observer window. On the other side of the window pass your thoughts as though they are cars on a road. Stay on the Observer side of the window, watching your thoughts move.

Write about being a passive, alert Observer.

Take a step back, watching your thoughts with greater detachment. Your Observer watches your thoughts but doesn't think your thoughts. Identify with your Observer and simply watch your thoughts move through your head for ten minutes.

Write about your experience.

You are not your thoughts.

You are not the thinker of your thoughts.

You simply are.

Just be.

And write about your experience.

You are not your feelings. Practice detachment and watch your feelings from behind the Observer window. Notice how they move and change when you practice presence and allow.

You are not the feeler of your feelings.

You simply are.

Just be.

Write about your experience.

Move into your Observer. Practice focusing your attention. Experience being you with focused attention for one second.

And for one more second.

And for one more second.

And then repeat.

Write about your experience.

Watch your thoughts and the thinker of your thoughts from a distance.

Watch your feelings and the feeler of your feelings from a distance.

Write about your experience.

How is watching your thoughts (and the thinker of your thoughts) different from watching your feelings (and the feeler of your feelings)?

Write about your experience watching your thoughts and the thinker of your thoughts and watching your feelings and the feeler of your feelings.

When you practice presence and you identify with your Observer, you look behind your thoughts and behind your feelings. Practice staying in your detached Observer, looking behind your thoughts and your feelings. Focus on the process of observing, not on what is observed.

Write about your experience.

What decisions do you notice behind your thoughts? If you're not sure, keep observing from a greater distance.

What beliefs do you notice behind your feelings? Stay present and focused.

Write about your experience.

When we commit to allowing transformation, we rest on the foundation of stillness that lies deeper in us than our thoughts or our feelings.

In our stillness, we allow.

We practice availability by practicing presence and passive receptivity. We trust the wisdom of our intuitive guidance.

Write about your experience.

Practice stillness throughout the day, paying attention to the second. Stop every hour for one second and notice.

Write about your experience.

We practice presence when we sit in meditation. We also practice presence when we watch ourselves, without judgment, move through our day. We practice presence when we notice our reactions without owning them. We practice presence when we accept what the day brings and we say, "Thank you."

Today practice presence.

Write about your experience.

KNOWING YOUR INNER WORLD

You have an Observer, neutral and detached. Your Observer simply notices *whatever is* without comment. Practice moving into your Observer at will.

Your Observer stands behind the Observer window. Your thoughts and feelings move past on the other side of the Observer window.

Stay in your Observer behind the Observer window. When you find that you think your thoughts instead of noticing your thoughts, you have moved out from behind the Observer window. Gently pull yourself back into the Observer position.

Practice this exercise ten times today and write about your experience.

When we stay in our Observer, we watch. We don't understand. We can't explain. And we can't predict. In our inner world, we are not in control. We only observe.

Today observe the activity in your inner world. Notice your thinking and label your thoughts. Notice your feelings and label your feelings.

Write about what you notice and the act of noticing.

Which parts of yourself did you dislike and try to ignore in your early life? (your feelings, your sensitivity, your rage, your quirkiness, your aggression, your fear, something else?)

How did you damage yourself in the process?

Do you damage yourself today? How?

Write your observations, thoughts, feelings, memories, associations, anything that comes to mind.

How have the "unwanted" parts of you grown up or remained the same?

How has your attitude toward them shifted?

Write about your experience of not wanting to own some parts of you.

Which traits and qualities have remained the same in you over many years and which have changed?

With which parts of yourself are you comfortable now? When do you easily and appropriately identify with them and let them carry you?

Write about your longstanding internal conflicts and their resolution or lack of resolution. What conflicts still challenge you?

Write about your experience and your thoughts.

What parts of you do you avoid, either intentionally or without conscious decision? (your anger, your passivity, your assertion, your surrender, your ambition, your joy, your vulnerability?)

Have you noticed that sometimes you need them? What do you do then?

Talk with and listen to each part of you that you resist. Keep the dialogue moving until a new understanding and a more accepting relationship evolves.

Write about your inner world experience and your outer world experience after your dialogues with your inner world aspects.

When you find some part of you taking a remark personally and feeling offended, just notice. As you stay in your Observer behind the Observer window, watch the dynamics among the different parts of you. How does the Frustrated Teenager handle offense? How does the Neglected Infant respond? What does the Earth Mother do? the Bully? the lonely Child? the mature Adult?

Write about what you notice and what you feel in each part of you.

Stay in your Observer behind the Observer window. Practice detachment, noticing a part that takes offense. And notice an empowered part of you that genuinely doesn't feel offended.

Can you move between the two parts of you at will?

What do you release in order to move between the two parts of you?

Write about your experience.

Do you usually identify with one part of yourself while disregarding another part which might be more suited to respond in a particular situation?

With which part of you do you find yourself identifying? Which part do you disregard?

Write about your experience. Notice patterns with this same aspect of you repeating its usual thinking and behavior.

When does this pattern work to support you and when does it not? Write about your experience.

Notice your critical self-talk. What does your Inner Critic say to you regularly?

Stay behind the Observer window and watch your Inner Critic. What do you notice about this figure?

Write about your experience in relation to your Inner Critic.

How long have you been aware of it?

How has it influenced you?

Can you hear its words without reacting?

Write about what you notice when you stand behind the Observer window and watch the Inner Critic.

Which part of you do you need but you don't usually call on? Your Moderator? Your Peacemaker? Your Debater? Your Forgiving Parent? Your General? Your Vulnerability?

Write about your experience without that part of you which you need.

What would it take to integrate this part of you?

Notice three empowered parts of you that don't take offense and notice how they respond in a particular situation:

Your Spiritual Warrior

Your Mature Adult

Your Caring Parent

Write about what each aspect of you contributes to your thinking and your choices.

What other empowered aspects exist in you?

Notice when you identify with an empowered aspect of you. Notice when you don't identify with an empowered aspect.

Write about using (or not using) your empowered aspects.

Know yourself in your most noble version. Today when another part of you arises – the Needy Child, the Lonely Adolescent, the Frustrated Artist – stay in your most noble version and respond to the other part of you from your better self.

Do this every time you need to for a week.

And write about it.

Appreciate one part of you that you usually don't appreciate.

What part of you is that?

Sit with that part of you and write about your experience being present and attentive to this part of you.

By opening to this part of you, do you recognize its gift for you?

Think of three people who irritate you. Notice their irritating qualities in your mind's movie.

These folks reflect something about yourself to you. What irritating "something" in you needs to be integrated?

Write about your experience considering this.

What is true about you that you don't particularly like?

Change your attitude toward this part of you. Sit with it. Get to know it. Listen to it. Accept it. Integrate it.

Then write.

When are you identified with your compassionate, confident Adult? How do you feel living from that part of you?

When are you identified with another, less powerful, less mature part of you? What part of you is that? How do you feel living from that part of you?

When you want to shift into your compassionate, confident Adult, how do you do that?

Write about moving into your compassionate, confident Adult and living from that part of you, in terms of your inner world, your relationship with yourself, and your relationships with others.

THE CONTROLLER

The Controller is the part of you that tells you how you should act. Get to know your Controller objectively.

Is your Controller male or female or something else?

List three Controller traits which you practice regularly.

When do you use your Controller appropriately and appreciate it?

Write about how your Controller serves you.

Your Controller hates vulnerability. How does that Controller attitude manifest in you?

Write about resisting your vulnerability.

How does your Controller avoid experiencing your feelings? Overeating, drinking alcohol, working compulsively, talking excessively?

This week notice when your Controller is prominent. Write about what you notice in your heart and in your head and in your muscles when your Controller is prominent.

What is your Controller's most frequent message to you?

How do you feel when you receive that message?

What do you do?

Notice when your Controller pops us inappropriately this week.

(When your Controller makes remarks about your worth as a person or about your experience, your Controller operates inappropriately.)

What's your relationship with your Controller?

In truth, your Controller is a damaged child behind an overbearing facade. The next time your Controller asserts her will, look for the hurting Child.

Write about what you notice and what you experience.

Which parts of you does your Controller fear/hate? (your sensitivity, your hurt, your neediness, your longing, your dreaming?)

Which parts of you does your Controller admire?

How does your Controller squelch your creativity?

How does your Controller influence your thinking and your judgment daily?

Write about your experience living with your Controller over decades.

Are there other parts of you? a playful Child? a sad Infant? an angry Adolescent? an idealistic Reformer? a Jock? a Joker? a Sociopath? a super-responsible Worker? an Earth Mother? an Artist? an Addict? a Trouble-maker?

Write about three parts of you, when you notice their influence in your thinking, and when you open to them.

Are you comfortable moving into your Controller? And out of your Controller? How do you do that? (Notice your self-talk and your muscle tension.)

PRACTICING SURRENDER

Surrender is the opposite of defeat. When we surrender, we adopt a humble stance. We pay attention.

We trust that we will be shown our next step.

We practice availability while we wait attentively.

And we say "Yes" to whatever moves through us.

Are you open to practicing surrender?

Write your reaction to reading these words.

We don't judge anything inside us when we practice surrender. Just for today practice not judging anything inside or outside you.

Write about your experience.

When we practice surrender, we accept *whatever is*. We may experience fear or pain or rage. But in our surrendered state, we remain behind the Observer window. We observe and experience at the same time.

Practice that every day.

And write about your experience.

When we surrender, we don't have an agenda or a goal. We don't judge anything we notice moving through us. We practice presence until the intensity of the experience diminishes.

This week practice staying present to your experience until it shifts naturally.

And write about it.

What is it like to resist nothing?

What do you need to release in order to practice non-resistance?

Practice non-resistance inside you and outside you for a week and write about your experience every day.

Notice what happens in your relationships when you practice non-resistance and when you don't take offense.

Write about what you notice.

Can you sit in stillness and watch everything that moves on the other side of the Observer window? When we practice surrender we say "Yes" to everything we notice and experience. Do this exercise for twenty minutes twice today.

Write about your experience practicing surrender.

When we allow, we don't know what will happen or what we'll feel. We simply stay behind the Observer window, noticing and and experiencing. What in you resists doing this?

Write what you notice about your experience and your resistance.

Life knows better than your intellect what your next step in healing and growth is. Today trust Life and notice what happens both inside you and outside you.

Write about your experience.

What is it like moving through the day, not looking through your Controller's eyes?

What part of you dominates when your Controller steps back?

Write about living today in the present without emphasis on the future or the past or your thoughts or your feelings.

Today, acknowledge that a Wisdom greater than your intellect's lives in you.

At the end of today write about your experience.

CONSCIOUSNESS

Consciousness, simply defined, is the is-ness of being. Deeper than your thoughts and your feelings is your being. We are vibrational beings, so in every second change is possible.

We don't need to look around or read a hundred books or listen to authorities. We just need to peer deeply inside ourselves, focusing on what it is to be us this second.

How does it feel to be you this second?

Write about being you right now.

In each second we practice a vibratory frequency without knowing that we do so. Our decision to ignore some parts of ourselves affects our vibratory frequency. Our decision to think instead of feel our feelings affects our vibratory frequency.

Every decision and every judgment, conscious and unconscious, affects our vibration.

Look back over your first six years. Notice the child who still lives in you.

What does s/he feel?

Notice what decisions and feelings affect his/her vibratory practice.

Write about what you notice.

How is your Inner Child the same today as s/he was when s/he was six?

Write your responses.

What does s/he want?

Listen and write about the feelings and thoughts you receive.

How does the world look to this child?

Write what you notice from this child's viewpoint.

What subtle, unconscious decision did you make in the first six years of life?

How did that decision affect your vibrational practice?

Write what you realize.

How is that decision still alive in you, affecting your vibrational practice and your life today?

Write as long as you can.

We don't need to _do_ anything. We need to notice our vibrational practice in the second. We don't even need to understand it. We just need to experience it.

Be aware of your vibrational practice. Stop five times today and notice what vibration you practice.

Write about what you notice.

Life knows what we need to acknowledge or to release to heal our vibrational practice. We simply tune in. We pay attention to *what is* this second inside us. Move into your Observer and notice *what is* this second. Keep observing and paying attention for thirty minutes.

Then write about your experience.

Do this exercise daily.

How do your childhood beliefs and distortions influence your vibratory practice today?

Write your responses and memories.

Today make a decision from your mature Adult about how you want to move through the day.

All day check in and notice if you honor that decision.

Write about your experience.

Closing down on our aliveness happens subtly. Move into your Observer and notice your lifespan over decades. Stay in your detached Observer and watch the tape of your life play.

Notice the decision points where you (unconsciously) chose to close down on your aliveness.

Notice how you close down on your aliveness today. Watch yourself in three recent memories. Notice what happens in your observable behavior and in your vibratory practice.

Write about closing down on your aliveness unconsciously.

SPIRITUAL WARRIOR

Anchoring in your deepest center becomes the daily goal for your life as a Spiritual Warrior. Not many of us choose "Spiritual Warrior" as our life orientation initially but after we write in our journals and meditate and see patterns in our encounters and reconsider our old choices and allow ourselves to be guided, we realize that our work is interior. Always interior. We very humbly acknowledge that our inner world presents the playground for our dynamic investigations.

Everything we need to see lives in us this second and everything we need to do starts with an inner world experience. While it may be (self-righteously) distracting to pursue outer world goals, activity often obfuscates our true focus. Practicing vibrational alignment with our deepest center by necessity requires stillness, attention, and a willingness to be shown.

We come to this work with an attitude of "I'm available." We don't know what we will learn or how, so we consider everything that crosses our path. Eventually, we recognize our directional markers, the heart tugs or thoughts we can't ignore. Maybe words come to us or an image in a dream sparks our imagination. We notice correlations between our inner world challenges and our outer world experiences.

And we realize that we're working in one tapestry. Outer and inner, it's all the same. No pointing fingers, no bad guys. We're not victims. Good doesn't contrast with evil. We're aware or not aware, responsible or not responsible. But we're never off the hook. We're looking at ourselves when we dislike others, when we take a position, and when we judge. We always come back to ourselves. The work is always interior.

And it never ends.

Write your reaction.

Are you willing to spend time in your inner world this week? Write for an hour when you can, not filtering anything. Tear up your pages at the end of the hour and sit in meditation for 30 minutes.

Journal and meditate every day this week.

Write what you notice.

Notice your resistance today. What do you resist? How do you resist? What's the common theme among your resistances?

How does your resistance to knowing your inner world reflect your resistance to life? What is behind your resistance?

Write your responses and associations.

When are you out of integrity with others?

When are you out of integrity with yourself?

This week every day ask yourself, "Am I practicing alignment with my deepest center?"

Write about moving out of alignment and back into alignment.

When do you let yourself off the hook?

What do you lose by allowing that?

What are your favorite excuses?

Write your responses and observations.

How are you with commitments to yourself? Nothing surpasses the importance of committing to yourself in your deepest center. Being a Good Parent to yourself means being aware of your needs, your feelings, and your patterns of resistance. At the same time your eyes fix on the practice of allowing transformation. Your Good Parent always holds your ultimate good as your intention and daily alignment as your practice.

Write your reactions to these words.

This week notice how you keep your commitments to yourself.

And write.

Not every part of you consistently chooses alignment with your deepest center. What parts of you resist practicing vibrational alignment?

"I notice my resistance when I eat when I'm not hungry."

"I notice resistance when I can't get focused and finish the task at hand."

"I notice resistance when I'd rather clean house than do my journal writing."

When do you notice resistance?

What form does it take?

Write about how you respond to resistance when you identify it.

Practicing vibrational alignment is momentary. We set aside time each day to practice vibrational alignment but we notice little upsets and distractions which capture our attention and seem to offer us something that feels better immediately. What shortcuts tempt you?

Chocolate?

A talkative neighbor?

The gossip at work?

Watching television?

These are all fine activities but we never want to lose our anchor in our deepest center. Write in your journal about your distractions. And then write about practicing vibrational alignment.

Practicing vibrational alignment anchors you in your deepest center. You don't align with an affirmation or someone else's words or an image of how you wish you appear. Alignment involves practicing presence and surrender and trust.

You practice presence when you stop and say, "What is it to be me this second?"

You practice surrender when you say, "I'm available to experience any feeling that comes. There is no place inside me I won't go."

You practice trust when you say, "I don't know where I'm being taken or what I will be shown but I know life pulls me to healing."

Practice presence, surrender, and trust today.

And write about it.

PARTNERING WITH LIFE

Most of us learn the same lesson repeatedly, only at greater and greater depth.

What is the area of your greatest challenge?

What are you learning?

What is your resistance?

Write your responses and associations.

How can you let this repetitive lesson be fun? Maybe treat it as an adventure for your inspired Investigator? Life works with you and plays with you.

Play with life today and write about your experience.

When you dance with life, life always leads. Life seems to draw you to certain experiences for a reason you don't understand. What does life seem to want you to experience this week?

What is the lesson behind the experience?

Write about your experience at the end of your days this week. Notice what you are learning and what you are releasing.

Days that creep by allow us to listen. Days that fly by encourage us to pay attention in the second. But with both days we anchor in our own vibrational alignment. Our truth is within. It's not a matter of making a relationship work. Or earning accolades. Or competing. It's always a matter of paying attention and moving deeper inside.

Today be still and listen to your own truth.

And write about your experience.

Trusting life to guide us implies an always-humble attitude. We don't need approbation from another person. We're never complete and we're continually learning. We don't indulge in interpersonal drama. We're not seeking distractions from ourselves. We just be.

Today be and notice.

Write about your experience trusting and noticing.

We acknowledge our partner, life, today. We consciously commit to paying attention. We know that we are not in charge and that today is not just another opportunity to force our will. We attune to receive the subtle gifts that life offers us.

After paying attention to your partner, life, for several hours write about your experience.

If today doesn't have a to-do list but it's simply a time for you to play at allowing, notice what today brings you.

When you sit in silence, notice how you feel.

Find an adjective to describe your thoughts.

Peer into your inner world as though you are exploring territory you've never walked.

And then write about your experience.

For the next hour, only take action after you have received an inner world impulse. Until then be still and attentive and wait.

Write about what it's like to pay attention to your inner world and to trust.

Has life carried you in directions you didn't choose? And not in directions you did?

What has been one over-arching theme of your life experience?

What have you learned about yourself?

Write your responses and associations.

What is important to you now? Integrity? Sincerity? Compassion? Toughness? Wealth? Intimidating others? Detachment?

Write about a quality you value and about your practice of that quality.

What was important to you in years now passed that you have released?

What else would you like to release? A tendency to close off your feelings? Fear of being known? Moving into anger too quickly? Accepting depression as natural? Resisting some parts of yourself?

Write about your thoughts and associations.

What ruts have you lived in without noticing that you chose limitation for yourself?

Write about your (unconsciously) chosen limitations.

Have you avoided sincere contacts with strangers or family or someone else? How is avoidance limiting you?

What's your choice about continuing your avoidance?

Write your responses.

Does life seem like an ordeal to be tolerated? A party to entertain you? An opportunity to experience your oneness with Spirit? A lonely journey?

Write about your experience.

Write about your experience and your expectations from the viewpoint of three parts of you.

And then from your Spiritual Warrior.

What do you do daily that doesn't serve you?

What thoughts do you practice regularly that don't serve you?

What old feelings do you continue to practice long past the time to release them?

All day notice and release.

Then write about your experience.

Have you avoided feeling vulnerable when others are around?

Take a risk and share your vulnerability.

Or simply be aware of your vulnerability, experience it, and write about it.

What is it you don't want anyone to know about you?

Do you want to continue that practice or are you ready to release that self-imposed limitation?

Write about your fears and expectations.

How do you maintain a low-level depression?

Write all your associations.

Do you tell yourself it's acceptable to live without passion?

Write about that.

How do you sabotage yourself with your thinking?

Do you tell yourself, "That's unrealistic. Forget it."?

Upon what dreams have you foreclosed?

Write about your associations.

YOUR SACRED DUTY

In our young years we learned to ignore a part of us, but as adults we can't live fully without welcoming every part of us home. That is your sacred duty. Welcome some part of you which you have dismissed.

What part of you is that?

Write about attending to this part of you now. What do you notice? What does this part want?

Staying stuck is the compromise between doing what you feel pulled to do and resisting what you fear might ensue. In what area are you stuck?

Write about it.

How will you take a small step today toward getting unstuck?

Write about your experience.

In what area have you relinquished wanting the best for yourself?

Write about it.

Do you want to reclaim your desire for the best for yourself?

Write about that.

How do you betray yourself?

Write about it.

Notice your thoughts and your feelings as they move through you. Label them (resenting, planning, remembering, judging, appreciating).

Which do you easily release and which do you wrestle with?

Write about how you keep the struggle going.

Noticing your thoughts from your detached Observer perspective allows you to acknowledge your thoughts without thinking your thoughts.

Practice that.

What do you notice?

What's behind your thoughts? A feeling you don't want to feel?

Write for as long as you can.

Noticing your feelings from your detached Observer perspective allows you to acknowledge your feelings without identifying with them.

What do you notice?

What's behind your feelings?

Write as long as you can.

What challenges you about practicing stillness and looking at your thoughts without thinking your thoughts?

And noticing your feelings without identifying with your feelings?

Write all your associations.

Behind your feelings lives one or more beliefs. What beliefs live in you deeper than your feelings?

Notice how those beliefs influence your experience in different circumstances.

Write about what you notice.

Move into the Observer position. Notice how it feels to be in the Observer position.

Stay in the Observer position, pulling your attention back when you think your thoughts instead of looking at your thoughts.

Practice paying attention to this second.

All the time, practice surrender which is saying, "Thank You," no matter what you feel or what happens.

Write about your experience.

Simply staying in your Observer behind the Observer window invites Life to pull you to healing. Life always responds supportively. We may not understand Life's response initially so we move behind the Observer window and we pay attention to the seconds of our day.

Write about your experience doing so — your resistance, your surprise, your insights, your trust.

What is a belief that you hold about yourself that you won't tell anyone?

What belief about yourself influences your ability to finish projects?

What is your belief about yourself regarding success?

Write all your associations.

What is your belief about receiving love?

About giving love?

About trusting love?

Write all your associations.

Do you want to change one of your deeply held beliefs about yourself?

Which one?

With what belief will you replace it?

Practice the vibration of the chosen belief consciously eight times today.

Notice your experience.

Notice your resistance.

Write about your experience and your resistance.

It's not what you say that invites experiences; it's the vibratory frequency that you practice. Your beliefs influence your vibration.

You may say that you're open to experiencing love and financial reward and joy, but the vibratory frequency which you practice determines your openness.

You can tell what vibration you practice by looking around you. Say, "Yes, I have created my life today, just the way it is, by my vibrational practice."

How does that feel?

What do you notice about your vibrational practice when you look around you?

Write your associations.

Sometimes you notice a vibratory practice in another which you don't recognize as operating in yourself.

If you have a strong reaction to another person, you are seeing yourself in them.

List examples of when you practice (consciously or unconsciously) the vibration that you notice and dislike in another person.

Write about what you notice and experience.

Sometimes we just want to be comfortable. That's our Controller telling us to close down on our experience. "Don't feel too much. Don't look too deeply. Just be happy."

But happiness isn't avoidance of who we are. Happiness results from allowing every part of ourselves to be.

Write your reactions and associations.

Think of the different parts of yourself as your children. Some of them need attention and care to grow up. Some need to be nurtured and drawn out. Some need to reconsider their choices.

Talk to and listen to three parts of yourself this week. Choose a part of you that you dislike — your Critic or your always needy Infant or your Victim or your Controller. Get to know that part of you. What does it want and what does it fear?

What belief underlies that part's thinking?

Write all your associations.

Look around you at what you have unconsciously created. What are three adjectives which describe your:

relationships _____, _____, _____

finances _____, _____, _____

health _____, _____, _____

expectations _____, _____, _____

joy _____, _____, _____

play _____, _____, _____

commitments _____, _____, _____

work _____, _____, _____

interests _____, _____, _____

When you step into your detached Observer and look at your life from the other side of the Observer window, what do you notice?

What is true about the life you create daily?

What is one part of you that would like a different experience?

How much of your time and attention does this part of you get?

Write.

Are you in awe of the opportunity you have been given to grow into yourself and to express yourself? You can be any version of yourself that you choose. And choose you always do, even if it's unconsciously. Each day you can choose to relive your consciousness of the past or to move into a more open, more loving, more accepting consciousness. No external restrictions limit you. This is totally about your consciousness and you are an independent operator in that area. We are not Victims or Whiners or Losers unless we choose to be.

Take full responsibility for your life today.

And write about that.

Live from your most noble self for six hours. Meet challenges directly and verbally but not abusively. Check in with your Spiritual Warrior every hour.

Then write about your experience.

What does contributing to the greater good mean to you? Is it you sharing yourself as you normally function?

Or is it you sharing yourself from your Spiritual Warrior?

How are the two different?

Write your responses and your thoughts and your associations.

This week notice your first thought upon awakening each day. How does that influence your experience of the day?

If you consciously choose your first thought each day, what would it be?

Practice consciously choosing your first thought every day for a week and write about your experience.

If you committed to living your best life now, what would you change?

What would you do?

Write about living your best life now. And any resistance to doing so.

Is some limitation from an earlier time still influencing your thinking?

Are you ready to let it go?

What would that take?

Write about your experience of letting go and allowing healing in this area.

What's your favorite self-destructive behavior? When do you choose to engage in it?

You've done this for years. Are you ready to take the next step and move past it?

Write about practicing self-destructive behaviors and your experience of releasing them.

What challenges you about practicing total self-acceptance?

What are the limits of your self-acceptance today?

Write about your experience of self-acceptance.

At what age in your early life did you learn self-acceptance or lack of self-acceptance?

How are you still functioning and thinking at that age level?

Write your memories, thoughts, associations, and feelings.

What did you substitute for acceptance by others and self-acceptance? Approval, achievement, money, power, food, alcohol, drugs, success?

How are you less than totally self-accepting?

Write about your inner world experience with self-acceptance and your blocks to self-acceptance.

Do you think self-acceptance is your responsibility?

Write about your awareness of self-acceptance.

What is something you really, really want?

Let yourself know that.

If you are willing, see yourself with that dream fulfilled.

Practice that "dream fulfilled" vibration every day.

Write about your experience.

What keeps you from being wildly enthusiastic about living your life?

Write about that.

If you were a better friend to yourself, what would you do differently?

How would you think differently?

How would you feel differently?

Write all your associations.

A version of _you_ needs to be your ideal. Write about the Ideal You.

How you think

How you feel

How you act

Moving through your day in your Spiritual Warrior, release one behavior or thought that you now practice and adopt one new self-affirming behavior or thought.

Write about your experience.

We play with our own consciousness. But we see our play manifest in our outer world. What do you notice around you that tells you something about your consciousness?

Your living space?

Your car?

Your record keeping?

Your refrigerator?

Your closet?

Notice and write.

Practicing partnership with life varies over time. What does practicing partnership with life today imply that you notice today?

Meditate.

And then write.

Your consciousness affects your experience today. Write about how.

You can shift your consciousness with your attention. How do you want to shift your consciousness? To what will you shift your attention?

Write about your experience.

Don't change your behavior today. Change an attitude. Choose to love some part of yourself unconditionally and notice how that affects your relationships.

Write about that.

Spend one day thinking only accepting thoughts about yourself and everyone else. Catch yourself when a critical thought slips in and affirm your accepting thoughts.

Write about your experience.

PRACTICING PEACE

Your consciousness, not your work position, lays the foundation for your power. Consciousness is the field in which you operate. You affect your total life experience by working with your consciousness. Your consciousness is your greatest contribution to the world.

When you meditate this week, notice what impacts your consciousness. Always look behind the details and the circumstances. Practice vibrational alignment with your deepest center.

And write.

Notice that your consciousness is not about you as an individual but you as being. It's your way of participating in the whole of humanity.

Today practice peace for one second.

Or more if you want.

Write from your consciousness of being.

What you do isn't as important as your vibrational practice.

Your personality isn't as important as your essence.

Today focus on your essence more than on your thoughts or feelings. Perceive from your essence. Respond from your essence. Decide from your essence.

Write about your experience.

Regardless of circumstances, practicing peace is our daily challenge. Are you willing to practice peace daily? Or not?

Write about your commitment to practice peace daily or your resistance to making this commitment.

Practicing peace does not imply denial of how you are this second. You don't need to change anything about you. In your meditation, look at yourself through compassionate, detached eyes.

What do you notice?

Write from your detached, compassionate Adult.

Practicing peace implies seeing no adversaries. Are you willing to do that?

What inside you is your adversary?

And what is the gift hidden in this part of you?

Write about your experience.

You are an eternal being. This particular lifetime casts its own particular shade but this lifetime is not the extent of your being. Perhaps you are struggling with addiction, severe limitation, or deviance.

Today be aware of your essence and not the details of this lifetime that frustrate you.

Accept, allow, and appreciate today's experience.

Write.

Healing is unlimited. But healing starts with consciousness. Don't imagine yourself healed. Just practice the vibration you will practice naturally and easily when you live immersed in your healed consciousness.

Write about your experience.

Operating from your healed consciousness envelops forgiveness, acceptance, and unconditional love. Your healed consciousness exists right now. Allow yourself to move into your healed consciousness and out from it at will.

Practice moving into your healed consciousness when you find you have left it without realizing what you were choosing.

Write about your experience.

There is not so much you need to do. Don't focus on behavior; focus on being. You can't will "aligned being" but you can allow it.

Practice allowing an experience of aligned being, especially when your thoughts carry you into alienated spaces.

Breathe and be.

Write about your experience of moving into alignment.

When you practice vibrational alignment, you have nothing to lose. You cannot be threatened. Whatever exists becomes more acceptable and less restricting.

Today practice being satisfied with *what is* this second.

Write about your experience.

When you lack clarity, experience being unclear and unable to move and let that be OK. Being still may be the perfect thing to do in the moment.

Practice stillness.

Pay attention.

Write about your experience.

Today defer to a wisdom greater than your mind's. Be aware of your partnership with that wisdom all day.

Write about your experience.

Practice gentleness with yourself and with others today.

Write about your experience.

What have you kept yourself away from? A dream? A feeling? Your spontaneity?

Allow yourself to move into that part of you.

Write about your experience.

Accept that the way you remember your past may not be the way it happened or the way anyone else remembers it.

Create a new past for yourself. This time everything works out beautifully. You grow up knowing you are wanted and valued.

Today practice the vibration of a person without any baggage.

Write about your experience.

Today be aware of your unlimitedness.

www.ingramcontent.com/pod-product-compliance
Ingram Content Group UK Ltd.
Pitfield, Milton Keynes, MK11 3LW, UK
UKHW041951230426
12048UKWH00008B/260